SUPER STEM CAREERS

A Day at Work with a
GEOLOGIST

AMELIA LETTS

PowerKiDS
press.

New York

Published in 2016 by The Rosen Publishing Group, Inc.
29 East 21st Street, New York, NY 10010

First Edition

Editor: Caitie McAneney
Book Design: Katelyn Heinle

Photo Credits: Cover Robbie Shone/Aurora/Getty Images; cover, pp. 1, 3, 4, 6–12, 14–18, 20, 22–24 (topographic vector design) Dancake/Shutterstock.com; p. 5 Photodiem/Shutterstock.com; p. 6 Natursports/Shutterstock.com; p. 9 Hero Images/Getty Images; p. 10 https://upload.wikimedia.org/wikipedia/commons/a/af/Geologists-tools_hg.jpg; p. 11 https://upload.wikimedia.org/wikipedia/commons/f/f1/VNIIOarctic.jpg; p. 13 (top) arek_malang/Shutterstock.com; p. 13 (bottom) Cultura RM/David Burton/Cultura/Getty Images; p. 15 michaeljung/Shutterstock.com; p. 16 Konstantnin/Shutterstock.com; p. 17 Russell Curtis/Science Source/Getty Images; p. 19 Ken M Johns/Science Source/Getty Images; p. 21 (top) Radu Razvan/Shutterstock.com; p. 21 (bottom) https://upload.wikimedia.org/wikipedia/commons/8/87/Mudlogging.JPG; p. 22 Deborah Cheramie/E+/Getty Images.

Cataloging-in-Publication Data

Letts, Amelia.
A day at work with a geologist / by Amelia Letts.
p. cm. — (Super STEM careers)
Includes index.
ISBN 978-1-5081-4406-9 (pbk.)
ISBN 978-1-5081-4407-6 (6-pack)
ISBN 978-1-5081-4408-3 (library binding)
1. Geology — Vocational guidance — Juvenile literature. 2. Geologists — Juvenile literature. I. Letts, Amelia. II. Title.
QE34.L467 2016
550.23—d23

Manufactured in the United States of America

CPSIA Compliance Information: Batch #BW16PK: For Further Information contact Rosen Publishing, New York, New York at 1-800-237-9932

CONTENTS

UNEARTHING A STEM CAREER

Geologists are scientists who study the earth. They look into what the earth was once like and what it's like today, and they even **predict** what will happen to it in the future. Geologists study the **materials** that make up the earth. They look at how the earth has changed and how it might change later.

Geologists do some work in a laboratory, but most of their work is in the field. That means they work outside and travel to new locations. There are many different areas of geology, and each one is a great example of "STEM," which stands for "science, **technology**, **engineering**, and math."

Geologists often need to take soil samples for testing. They aren't afraid to get dirty!

WHAT IS GEOLOGY?

Geology is a branch of science, which is the first part of STEM. That means geologists are a specialized kind of scientist. They study earth science to better understand the world we live in.

Just as geology is a branch of science, there are many branches of geology. Seismology is the study of **earthquakes**. Seismologists look at how, when, and where earthquakes happen to predict earthquakes in the future and hopefully keep people safe. Volcanology is the study of **volcanoes**. Volcanologists study volcanoes to learn about their history and possibly predict when they might erupt again. Hydrology is the study of flowing water on Earth's surface.

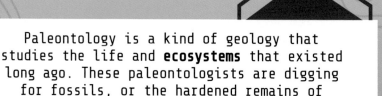

Paleontology is a kind of geology that studies the life and **ecosystems** that existed long ago. These paleontologists are digging for fossils, or the hardened remains of living things that existed long ago.

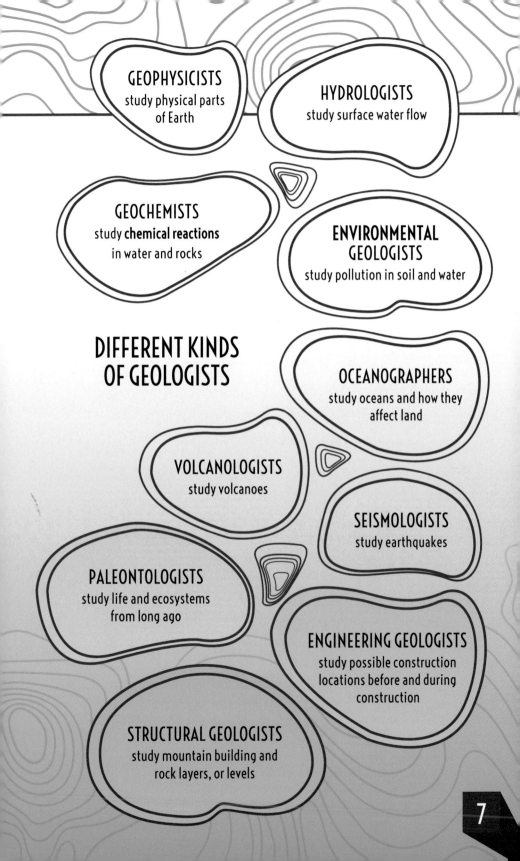

GEOPHYSICISTS
study physical parts of Earth

HYDROLOGISTS
study surface water flow

GEOCHEMISTS
study **chemical reactions** in water and rocks

ENVIRONMENTAL GEOLOGISTS
study pollution in soil and water

DIFFERENT KINDS OF GEOLOGISTS

OCEANOGRAPHERS
study oceans and how they affect land

VOLCANOLOGISTS
study volcanoes

SEISMOLOGISTS
study earthquakes

PALEONTOLOGISTS
study life and ecosystems from long ago

ENGINEERING GEOLOGISTS
study possible construction locations before and during construction

STRUCTURAL GEOLOGISTS
study mountain building and rock layers, or levels

COMBINING AREAS OF SCIENCE

Geologists often go to a four-year college for earth science or geology. Then, they pick their specialty. Some geologists combine geology with another branch of science, such as chemistry or physics.

Chemistry is the study of matter and the way it changes. Chemists often look at what matter is made of and what happens to matter when it mixes with other matter in different conditions. Geochemists study chemical reactions in water and rocks. Physics looks at the nature and properties of energy and matter. Geophysicists study the physical properties of matter, such as rock layers, and the forces working on it.

SUPER STEM SMARTS

Geophysicists observe what happens under Earth's surface. They study how landmasses move and change. They try to understand the forces that make this happen.

Geochemists collect samples of earth and test it. Some geochemists use their knowledge to discover areas rich with natural resources, such as minerals, oil, and gas.

GEOLOGY TOOLS

Geologists use many tools to do their job. Some jobs require basic tools, while others require the most advanced science technology available.

When a geologist is out in the field, they bring tools to collect samples and test the ground and water. A geologist may use a tool called a Brunton compass, or Brunton Pocket Transit, to help them find an exact location. To get a soil or groundwater sample, a geologist might use an earth drill to make holes in the ground. They often carry sample bags, which are waterproof, to hold soil and rock samples.

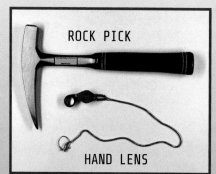

ROCK PICK

HAND LENS

Geologists use rock picks, which are hammers with a sharp, pointed tip for breaking rocks.

EXTREME LAB TECHNOLOGY

Science laboratories hold some of the most advanced technology. Geologists use computers to store information from the samples they take. They can use computers to make graphs and charts and to share information. They can **simulate** natural events, such as earthquakes and volcanic eruptions.

Sometimes, geologists use a tool called an electron microprobe. This device uses a charged beam to scan a piece of matter. It can tell a geologist what the sample is made of without harming the sample. This is an especially important tool in paleontology because the samples are very old and easily harmed.

Geologists use big tools called mass spectrometers to identify the type and amount of chemicals in a piece of matter.

13

ENGINEERING GEOLOGISTS

So far, we know that geologists like to observe and **analyze** matter, but are they involved in engineering things? Some geologists, called engineering geologists, help engineers and construction workers **design** and build things.

Before something can be built, it needs to have a safe and suitable location. Nothing is more important than the quality of the ground beneath a structure. Engineering geologists go to a construction site before anything is built. They look at the quality of the rock, water, and soil. They answer these questions: Is the rock hard enough? Will the soil crumble away with a rainstorm? Is it likely to flood?

Engineering geologists look at the designs for the structure that's being built. They make sure the structure's design is suitable for the location.

MATH MATTERS

If you want to be a geologist, it's important to have great math skills. Geologists use math when they're collecting and testing samples. They want to know the exact amount of matter they have. A geologist might use a scale or balance to measure a sample's mass. A correct measurement will help them figure how much of the sample is made up of certain **elements**.

Geologists also use math to create charts and graphs. This is important because these charts and graphs can help geologists look for patterns.

Patterns in data can help a geologist predict future events. For example, a seismograph measures the seismic, or earthquake, activity in an area and can help predict big earthquakes.

MAP MAKING

Math is an important part of making correct maps. Many geologists depend on maps to find an exact location for taking samples. For example, a paleontologist might use a map to arrive at an ancient lakebed to look for fossils. Geologists often use math when using a compass. They have to measure for declination, or the angle formed between a compass's magnetic needle and true north.

Geologists also create geophysical surveys, which are collections of data about the physical properties of an area. These charts show the exact locations of important features both above and below the ground.

It's important that geologists record the exact location where they've taken a sample. A location on Earth's surface is measured in latitude and longitude.

A CAREER IN GEOLOGY

Where do geologists work? By now, we know there are many different branches of geology. Some geologists, such as volcanologists and paleontologists, spend a lot of time working in the field. They might travel to volcanoes and fossil locations around the world. Other geologists spend more time in a lab testing samples.

Geologists may work for government agencies, such as the Environmental Protection Agency, National Park Service, and Bureau of Land Management. They might work for oil and mining companies, advising the company about where to drill or mine. Their jobs may be different, but they all use STEM!

SUPER STEM SMARTS

Many geologists work for engineering firms that want to build new structures.

Days as a geologist are never the same. There are always new places to visit and new ground to break!

BECOMING A GEOLOGIST

Do you like digging in the dirt? Do you like collecting rocks and minerals? Do you love finding fossils? You might be a geologist in the making!

Geologists have to attend a four-year college program in earth science or geology. Then, they might continue their education, focusing on a certain field of geology. Someone who's interested in keeping nature clean might study and work in environmental geology. Someone who's interested in volcanoes might decide to study volcanology.

Go outside and look around. What part of our world most interests you? Is it the mountains in the distance or the soil under your feet?

GLOSSARY

analyze: To study something deeply.

chemical reaction: A process in which the structure of the matter that makes up a substance is changed.

design: To create the plan for something. Also, the plan for something.

earthquake: A shaking of the ground caused by the movement of Earth's crust.

ecosystem: All the living things in an area.

element: Matter that's pure and has no other type of matter in it.

engineering: The use of science and math to build better objects.

environmental: Having to do with the natural world.

material: Something used to make something else.

predict: To guess what will happen in the future based on facts or knowledge.

simulate: To represent the operation of a process by means of another system.

technology: The way people do something using tools and the tools that they use.

volcano: An opening in a planet's surface through which hot, liquid rock sometimes flows.

INDEX

WEBSITES

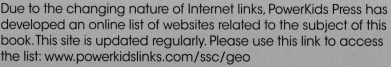

Due to the changing nature of Internet links, PowerKids Press has developed an online list of websites related to the subject of this book. This site is updated regularly. Please use this link to access the list: www.powerkidslinks.com/ssc/geo